Choosing Life:

Finding Meaning and Reasons to Stay Alive.

by

Alan S. Rodriguez

Introduction

Suicide is a complex and devastating issue that affects individuals, families, and communities around the world. According to the World Health Organization, approximately 800,000 people die by suicide each year, making it one of the leading causes of death globally. Despite the gravity of the situation, suicide remains a topic that is often stigmatized and shrouded in silence, making it difficult for individuals who are struggling to find the support and resources they need.

"Choosing Life: Finding Meaning and Reasons to Stay Alive" is a book that aims to break the silence and provide hope and guidance for those who are struggling with thoughts of suicide. This book is not just for individuals who have experienced suicidal thoughts, but also for family members, friends, and professionals who want to better understand and support those who may be at risk. The book is grounded in evidence-based research, as well as personal stories and experiences, to provide a comprehensive and compassionate guide for navigating the complex terrain of suicide prevention.

The book is organized into five chapters that cover a range of topics, including understanding the importance of choosing life, exploring your inner world, discovering your purpose, building a support system, and creating a sustainable plan for life. Each chapter offers practical tools, exercises, and resources that readers can use to cultivate a sense of meaning, purpose, and hope in their lives. Ultimately, the goal of "Choosing Life" is to empower individuals to recognize their own worth and potential, and to find the strength and resilience to stay alive.

Chapter 1

Understanding the Importance of Choosing Life

"Choosing life is not just about existing, it's about embracing every opportunity, cherishing every moment, and creating a purposeful journey towards a fulfilling future."

Understanding the importance of choosing life is the first step in suicide prevention. Suicide is a complex issue that is often driven by a sense of hopelessness and despair. People who are contemplating suicide may feel like they have no other option, that their problems are insurmountable, or that their life has no meaning or value. It's important to understand that suicide is not a choice, but rather a response to overwhelming emotional pain.

Choosing life is not just a decision, but a process. It involves recognizing that life is worth living, even in the midst of difficult circumstances. It requires cultivating a sense of hope and optimism, and finding reasons to continue living, even when things seem hopeless. This process can be challenging, but it's essential for anyone who is struggling with suicidal thoughts.

There are many reasons why choosing life is important. Suicide not only has a devastating impact on individuals and families, but it also affects entire communities. Choosing life can help prevent the loss of a valuable human life, and can also inspire others who may be struggling to find hope and meaning in their own lives. Ultimately, choosing life is about recognizing the inherent worth and value of every individual, and affirming the importance of life itself.

The impact of suicide on individuals, families, and communities

The impact of suicide is far-reaching, affecting not only the individual who dies, but also their loved ones and the wider community. Suicide can have a profound emotional, psychological, and social impact on those who are left behind, often leaving them struggling to make sense of their loss and to cope with the aftermath of the suicide.

For individuals who have lost a loved one to suicide, the grief and trauma can be intense and long-lasting. Survivors of suicide loss may experience a range of emotions, including shock, guilt, anger, and profound sadness. They may also struggle with feelings of isolation, stigma, and shame, as suicide is often stigmatized and misunderstood.

The impact of suicide is not limited to the immediate family and friends of the deceased, however. Suicide can also have a ripple effect throughout entire communities, affecting schools, workplaces, and other social institutions. Suicide can contribute to a sense of fear and insecurity, and can also lead to social isolation and division. It is therefore essential that suicide prevention is approached as a collective responsibility, involving a range of stakeholders and community members.

In conclusion, suicide is a complex and devastating issue that has a profound impact on individuals, families, and communities. By understanding the impact of suicide, we can better appreciate the need for prevention and support, and work toward creating a more compassionate and resilient society.

Recognizing warning signs and risk factors for suicide
Recognizing the warning signs and risk factors for suicide is crucial for early intervention and prevention. While everyone experiences distress and struggles at some point in their lives, some individuals may be at greater risk for suicidal thoughts and behaviors. It's important to be aware of the warning signs and risk factors associated with suicide, so that you can recognize when someone may be at risk and offer support.

Warning signs of suicide may include:

1. Talking about wanting to die or to kill oneself

2. Expressing feelings of hopelessness or being trapped
3. Increased substance use or reckless behavior
4. Extreme mood swings or withdrawal
5. Giving away belongings or saying goodbye to loved ones

Risk factors for suicide may include:

1. Previous suicide attempt(s)
2. Mental health disorders, such as depression, anxiety, or bipolar disorder
3. Substance abuse or addiction
4. Family history of suicide or mental health disorders
5. Trauma or abuse
6. Chronic illness or pain

It's important to note that not everyone who experiences these warning signs or risk factors will attempt suicide, and that suicide prevention is a complex and multifaceted issue. However, recognizing these signs and risk factors can help us better understand and respond to those who may be struggling with suicidal thoughts or behaviors, and can be a crucial step toward preventing suicide. If you or someone you know is struggling with suicidal thoughts or behaviors, it's important to seek help from a mental health professional or a crisis helpline.

Debunking common misconceptions about suicide

There are many misconceptions about suicide that can hinder our ability to prevent and respond to this complex issue. By debunking these myths and misconceptions, we can better understand the realities of suicide and work towards creating a more compassionate and supportive society.

Myth: People who talk about suicide are just seeking attention.

Fact: Talking about suicide is often a cry for help, and should be taken seriously. Ignoring or dismissing someone's suicidal thoughts or behaviors can have devastating consequences.

Myth: Suicidal people are selfish or weak.

Fact: Suicidal thoughts and behaviors are often driven by intense emotional pain and distress, and are not a sign of weakness or selfishness.

Myth: Suicide only affects certain types of people.

Fact: Suicide can affect anyone, regardless of age, gender, race, or social status.

Myth: Once someone has made a suicide attempt, they are unlikely to try again.

Fact: Previous suicide attempts are a significant risk factor for future attempts, and should be taken seriously.

Myth: Suicide is always the result of mental illness.

Fact: While mental illness is a common risk factor for suicide, there are many other factors that can contribute to suicidal thoughts and behaviors, including social isolation, relationship problems, financial difficulties, and trauma.

It's important to understand that suicide is a complex and multifaceted issue, and that there is no single cause or solution. By challenging these myths and misconceptions, we can better understand and respond to the realities of suicide, and work towards creating a more supportive and compassionate society for those who may be struggling.

Chapter 2

Exploring Your Inner World

"Exploring your inner world is like diving into the ocean of your own consciousness, discovering hidden treasures and unlocking the mysteries of your true self."

Exploring your inner world is a process of self-discovery that can help you better understand your thoughts, feelings, and behaviors. By exploring your inner world, you can gain insight into the unconscious patterns and beliefs that may be driving your emotions and actions, and develop greater self-awareness and self-acceptance.

One way to explore your inner world is through journaling. Writing down your thoughts and feelings in a journal can help you identify patterns and themes in your inner experience, and can provide a safe and private space for reflection and self-expression.

Meditation and mindfulness practices can also be helpful for exploring your inner world. By practicing mindfulness, you can learn to observe your thoughts and emotions without judgment, and develop greater awareness of the present moment.

Therapy and counseling can also be valuable tools for exploring your inner world. A trained therapist can provide a supportive and non-judgmental space for exploring your thoughts and feelings, and can help you develop strategies for managing difficult emotions and changing unhelpful patterns of behavior.

Ultimately, exploring your inner world is a deeply personal and ongoing process that requires patience, curiosity, and self-compassion. By developing a greater understanding of your inner experience, you can cultivate greater resilience, self-awareness, and emotional well-being.

Examining your thoughts and emotions

Examining your thoughts and emotions is a key aspect of self-awareness and personal growth. By taking a closer look at your thoughts and emotions, you can gain insight into your internal experiences and develop greater control over your reactions and behaviors.

One way to examine your thoughts and emotions is through mindfulness meditation. Mindfulness involves bringing your attention to the present moment, and observing your thoughts and emotions without judgment. By developing greater awareness of your thoughts and emotions, you can begin to identify patterns and themes in your internal experience, and develop greater control over your reactions and behaviors.

Another way to examine your thoughts and emotions is through cognitive-behavioral therapy (CBT). CBT is a type of therapy that focuses on identifying and changing negative thought patterns and behaviors. Through CBT, you can learn to recognize and challenge unhelpful thoughts, and develop more positive and adaptive ways of thinking and behaving.

Journaling can also be a helpful tool for examining your thoughts and emotions. By writing down your thoughts and feelings, you can gain a deeper understanding of your internal experience, and identify patterns and themes in your thinking and emotions.

Ultimately, examining your thoughts and emotions is an ongoing process that requires patience, curiosity, and self-compassion. By developing greater self-awareness, you can cultivate greater emotional intelligence, improve your relationships with others, and enhance your overall well-being.

Understanding the role of past experiences and traumas

Past experiences and traumas can have a significant impact on our thoughts, emotions, and behaviors. Unresolved trauma and negative past experiences can manifest in many ways, such as anxiety, depression, and difficulty forming healthy relationships.

Understanding the role of past experiences and traumas in shaping our internal experiences can be a powerful tool for healing and personal growth. By identifying and processing past traumas, we can begin to release the emotional and physical pain that they may be causing in our present lives.

There are many approaches to processing past traumas, including therapy, mindfulness practices, and somatic therapies. Therapy, in particular, can provide a supportive and safe space for exploring past traumas and developing coping strategies for managing the emotions and behaviors that may be related to them.

Mindfulness practices such as meditation and breathing exercises can also be helpful for processing past traumas. By bringing your attention to the present moment and observing your thoughts and emotions without judgment, you can develop greater awareness of the ways in which past traumas may be impacting your internal experience.

Somatic therapies such as yoga and body-based therapies can also be helpful for processing past traumas. These therapies focus on releasing emotional and physical tension that may be held in the body as a result of past traumas.

Ultimately, processing past traumas is a deeply personal and ongoing process that requires patience, self-compassion, and the support of others. By developing greater awareness and acceptance of the impact of past experiences on our present lives, we can begin to heal and move towards greater emotional and psychological well-being.

Practicing self-compassion and self-care

Practicing self-compassion and self-care is an essential aspect of maintaining emotional and psychological well-being. Self-compassion involves treating yourself with kindness, understanding, and acceptance, especially during difficult times. Self-care involves engaging in activities that nourish and replenish your physical, emotional, and spiritual energy.

One way to practice self-compassion is through self-talk. This involves speaking to yourself in a kind, compassionate, and supportive manner, as you would speak to a friend or loved one. By practicing self-talk, you can develop a more positive and accepting attitude toward yourself and your experiences.

Another way to practice self-compassion is through mindfulness practices such as meditation and breathing exercises. By bringing your attention to the present moment and observing your thoughts and emotions without judgment, you can develop greater self-awareness and self-acceptance.

Self-care involves engaging in activities that promote physical, emotional, and spiritual well-being. This may include activities such as exercise, healthy eating, getting enough sleep, spending time in nature, and engaging in hobbies or creative pursuits. By prioritizing self-care activities, you can recharge your energy and cultivate greater resilience and emotional balance.

Therapy and counseling can also be valuable tools for practicing self-compassion and self-care. A trained therapist can provide support and guidance for developing self-compassion practices, and can help you identify and prioritize self-care activities that are most effective for your individual needs.

Ultimately, practicing self-compassion and self-care is an ongoing process that requires patience, commitment, and self-awareness. By prioritizing your emotional and psychological well-being, you can cultivate greater resilience, self-acceptance, and overall happiness in your life.

Chapter 3

Discovering Your Purpose

"Discovering your purpose is like finding the missing puzzle piece that completes the picture of your life, giving meaning to your existence and guiding your path towards fulfillment."

Discovering your purpose in life can provide a sense of direction, fulfillment, and meaning. However, the process of uncovering your purpose can be challenging and may require a deep exploration of your values, passions, and strengths.

One way to begin exploring your purpose is to reflect on what brings you joy and fulfillment. This may involve identifying activities or experiences that you find particularly meaningful or engaging, such as volunteering, creating art, or working with others to achieve a common goal.

Another way to uncover your purpose is to identify your core values. Values are the principles and beliefs that guide your life, and can include things like integrity, compassion, and creativity. By identifying your core values, you can begin to align your life choices and actions with what is most important to you.

Strengths assessment tools can also be helpful for identifying your purpose. These tools can help you identify your unique strengths and talents, and provide guidance on how to apply them in your personal and professional life.

Exploring your purpose may also involve taking risks and trying new things. By stepping outside of your comfort zone and exploring new experiences, you may discover new passions and interests that align with your purpose.

Ultimately, discovering your purpose is an ongoing process that requires patience, curiosity, and self-awareness. By aligning your life choices and actions with your values, passions, and strengths, you can cultivate a sense of purpose and fulfillment in your personal and professional life.

Finding meaning and purpose in life

Finding meaning and purpose in life is a deeply personal and individual journey that can provide a sense of direction, fulfillment, and joy. While the process of uncovering meaning and purpose can be challenging, there are several strategies and approaches that can be helpful.

One way to find meaning and purpose in life is to connect with others and contribute to the well-being of your community. This may involve volunteering, participating in social activities, or working towards a common goal with others. By engaging in activities that allow you to make a positive impact on others, you may find a greater sense of purpose and fulfillment in your life.

Another approach to finding meaning and purpose is to explore your personal values and beliefs. Identifying your core values and beliefs can provide a sense of clarity and direction in your life, and can help you make choices that align with your deepest desires and motivations.

Self-reflection and introspection can also be helpful for uncovering meaning and purpose. This may involve journaling, meditation, or other mindfulness practices that allow you to connect with your inner self and explore your thoughts, feelings, and desires.

Creativity and self-expression can also be a powerful tool for finding meaning and purpose in life. Engaging in creative pursuits such as art, music, or writing can provide a sense of purpose and fulfillment by allowing you to express yourself in unique and meaningful ways.

Ultimately, finding meaning and purpose in life is an ongoing process that requires patience, self-awareness, and openness to new experiences. By exploring your values, connecting with others, and engaging in activities that bring you joy and fulfillment, you can cultivate a sense of purpose and meaning in your life.

Identifying your personal values and goals

Identifying your personal values and goals is an important step toward living a fulfilling and meaningful life. Personal values are the beliefs and principles that guide your behavior and decision-making, while goals are the specific outcomes or achievements you want to attain.

One way to identify your personal values is to reflect on what is most important to you in life. This may involve considering your relationships, your career aspirations, your spiritual beliefs, and your personal interests. Once you have identified your values, you can use them to guide your decision-making and actions, and ensure that you are living in alignment with what matters most to you.

Setting goals is another important step toward achieving a fulfilling and meaningful life. Goals can provide a sense of direction and motivation, and can help you make progress toward your desired outcomes. When setting goals, it's important to be specific, measurable, and realistic. This may involve breaking down larger goals into smaller, more achievable steps, and setting timelines for each step.

It's also important to regularly review and reassess your values and goals. Life is constantly changing, and what was important to you at one point in time may not be as relevant or meaningful to you later on. Regularly checking in with yourself and adjusting your values and goals as needed can help ensure that you are living a life that is true to yourself and aligned with your deepest desires and aspirations.

Ultimately, identifying your personal values and goals is an ongoing process that requires self-reflection, introspection, and a willingness to explore and try new things. By living in alignment with your values and pursuing meaningful goals, you can cultivate a sense of purpose and fulfillment in your personal and professional life.

Pursuing your passions and interests

Pursuing your passions and interests is a powerful way to add more meaning and fulfillment to your life. When you engage in activities that you enjoy and that are personally meaningful to you, you are more likely to experience a sense of purpose and satisfaction.

One way to pursue your passions and interests is to explore new hobbies and activities. This may involve trying out a new sport or physical activity, learning a new skill, or pursuing a creative endeavor such as painting, writing, or music. By trying out new things and pushing yourself out of your comfort zone, you may discover new passions and interests that you didn't even know existed.

Another way to pursue your passions and interests is to incorporate them into your daily life. This may involve finding ways to integrate your interests into your work, volunteering in a field that aligns with your passions, or simply making time for hobbies and activities that bring you joy and fulfillment. By making your passions and interests a priority in your life, you are more likely to feel a sense of purpose and happiness.

It's also important to recognize that pursuing your passions and interests is not always easy or straightforward. You may face challenges or setbacks along the way, and it may take time to find the right activities or hobbies that truly resonate with you. However, by persisting and staying true to yourself, you can cultivate a life that is rich in meaning and purpose.

Ultimately, pursuing your passions and interests is a valuable way to connect with your inner self, discover new strengths and abilities, and add more joy and fulfillment to your life. By making time for the activities and hobbies that truly matter to you, you can live a life that is true to yourself and aligned with your deepest desires and aspirations.

Chapter 4

Building a Support System

Building a support system is like constructing a sturdy bridge that helps you cross the turbulent waters of life, providing stability, strength, and comfort along the way."

Building a support system is a crucial step toward maintaining good mental health and well-being. A support system can provide emotional, practical, and social support during challenging times, and can help you feel connected and supported in your personal and professional life.

One way to build a support system is to identify the people in your life whom you can rely on for support. This may include close friends, family members, colleagues, or mental health professionals. Reach out to these individuals and let them know how they can support you during times of stress or difficulty. This may involve simply lending an ear to listen, offering practical assistance, or providing encouragement and motivation.

Another way to build a support system is to get involved in your community. Joining a club, organization, or community group can provide opportunities for social connection and support, and can help you build a sense of belonging and purpose. Volunteer work is also a great way to give back to your community and build meaningful connections with others.

It's also important to take care of yourself and practice self-care when building a support system. This may involve setting boundaries, practicing mindfulness, getting enough rest and exercise, and seeking out professional help when needed. By taking care of yourself, you can better support others and maintain healthy relationships.

Ultimately, building a support system is an ongoing process that requires effort and commitment. By reaching out to others, getting involved in your community, and practicing self-care, you can cultivate a network of support that can help you navigate life's challenges and experience greater joy and fulfillment.

Reaching out to friends, family, and professionals for help

Reaching out to friends, family, and professionals for help is a critical step in maintaining good mental health and well-being. It's important to remember that seeking help is not a sign of weakness, but rather a sign of strength and courage in acknowledging when you need support.

When reaching out to friends and family, it's important to be honest and open about your struggles and needs. This may involve initiating difficult conversations and asking for specific forms of support, such as someone to talk to or practical assistance with daily tasks. It's also important to respect others' boundaries and to understand that not everyone may be able to provide the level of support you need.

If you feel that you need professional help, it's important to seek out a mental health professional such as a therapist, counselor, or psychiatrist. These professionals can provide a safe and confidential space to explore your thoughts and feelings, develop coping strategies, and receive evidence-based treatment for mental health conditions.

There are also many resources available for those in crisis or in need of immediate support. Crisis hotlines, such as the National Suicide Prevention Lifeline (1-800-273-TALK), offer free and confidential support and can connect you with local resources and services.

Remember, seeking help is a brave and important step towards taking care of yourself and improving your mental health. By reaching out to friends, family, and professionals, you can receive the support and resources you need to navigate life's challenges and thrive.

Navigating social stigma and seeking support in a judgment-free zone

Navigating social stigma can be a challenge when seeking support for mental health issues. Unfortunately, there is still a great deal of stigma and shame surrounding mental illness in many communities, which can make it difficult to reach out for help.

One way to navigate this stigma is to seek out support in a judgment-free zone. This may involve finding a mental health professional or support group that specializes in your particular mental health concern or community. For example, there are many support groups and resources available specifically for individuals from marginalized or underrepresented communities, such as LGBTQ+ individuals, people of color, and those with disabilities.

It's also important to remember that you are not alone in your struggles. Many people experience mental health challenges at some point in their lives, and seeking help is a common and important step towards recovery. By sharing your experiences and connecting with others who have similar experiences, you can reduce feelings of isolation and build a sense of community.

If you encounter stigma or judgment from others when seeking support, it's important to remember that this is not a reflection of your worth or value as a person. Try to focus on your own needs and priorities, and seek out support from individuals or organizations that are welcoming and affirming of your experiences.

Ultimately, seeking support for mental health challenges is an act of self-care and a step towards improving your well-being. By navigating stigma and seeking support in a judgment-free zone, you can receive the care and resources you need to thrive and live a fulfilling life.

Joining support groups and other communities

Joining support groups and other communities can be a valuable resource for individuals navigating mental health challenges. Support groups can provide a safe and supportive space to share experiences, offer and receive advice, and build connections with others who may be going through similar struggles.

There are a wide variety of support groups available for different mental health concerns, including groups focused on anxiety, depression, bipolar disorder, eating disorders, addiction, and more. Many support groups are led by mental health professionals, while others may be peer-led by individuals who have personal experience with a particular mental health concern.

In addition to support groups, there are many other communities and organizations that can provide a sense of belonging and support. These may include religious or spiritual communities, LGBTQ+ groups, hobby or interest groups, and more. By connecting with others who share common interests or experiences, you can build a sense of community and reduce feelings of isolation.

When seeking out support groups and communities, it's important to find a group that is a good fit for your needs and preferences. This may involve attending several different groups before finding the right fit. It's also important to prioritize safety and ensure that the group is led by qualified professionals or trained facilitators.

Overall, joining support groups and other communities can be a powerful way to build connections and receive support while navigating mental health challenges. By connecting with others who have shared experiences, you can reduce feelings of isolation and build a sense of belonging and community.

Chapter 5

Creating a Sustainable Plan for Life

"Creating a sustainable plan for life is like planting a garden, nurturing it with care and attention, and enjoying the bountiful harvest that it yields for years to come."

Creating a sustainable plan for life is an important step toward achieving and maintaining mental health and wwell-being This involves developing a long-term plan that takes into account your personal values, goals, and resources, and sets realistic and achievable targets for yourself.

One key aspect of creating a sustainable plan for life is setting realistic goals that align with your personal values and priorities. This may involve identifying specific areas of your life that you would like to improve, such as your relationships, career, or physical health, and setting achievable targets that will help you move towards your goals over time.

Another important aspect of a sustainable plan for life is creating a daily routine that prioritizes self-care and mental health. This may involve developing healthy habits such as exercise, mindfulness meditation, and social connection, as well as setting boundaries and limits around work and other obligations.

In addition to setting goals and prioritizing self-care, it's important to seek out support and resources that can help you achieve your goals and maintain your mental health over the long-term. This may involve working with a mental health professional, joining a support group, or seeking out other resources such as books, podcasts, or online forums.

Ultimately, creating a sustainable plan for life is about developing a personalized roadmap that helps you achieve your goals while maintaining your mental health and well-being. By setting realistic goals, prioritizing self-care, and seeking out support and resources, you can build a fulfilling and sustainable life that aligns with your personal values and priorities.

Developing coping skills and resilience

Developing coping skills and resilience is an important part of maintaining mental health and well-being. Coping skills are techniques and strategies that can help individuals manage stress and difficult emotions, while resilience refers to an individual's ability to adapt and recover from adversity.

There are many different coping skills that can be helpful in managing stress and difficult emotions, including mindfulness meditation, deep breathing exercises, physical exercise, and talking with a trusted friend or mental health professional. It's important to identify coping skills that work well for you and to practice them regularly, so that they become a habit and can be easily accessed when needed.

Building resilience involves developing a positive mindset and a sense of purpose, as well as cultivating a strong support system. This may involve setting realistic goals, focusing on personal strengths and accomplishments, and seeking out support from family, friends, or mental health professionals.

In addition to developing coping skills and resilience, it's important to practice self-compassion and to be gentle with yourself during difficult times. This may involve reframing negative self-talk and focusing on self-care and self-compassion, such as taking time for rest and relaxation, engaging in activities that bring joy and fulfillment, and practicing gratitude and appreciation for the positive aspects of life.

Ultimately, developing coping skills and resilience is an ongoing process that requires patience, practice, and self-awareness. By prioritizing self-care, building a strong support system, and practicing positive coping skills, individuals can cultivate the resilience and inner strength needed to navigate life's challenges and maintain mental health and well-being.

Identifying potential triggers and strategies for managing them

Identifying potential triggers and developing strategies for managing them is an important part of maintaining mental health and well-being. Triggers are events or situations that can lead to feelings of stress, anxiety, or depression, and can vary widely from person to person.

One strategy for identifying triggers is to keep a journal or record of your emotions and experiences, noting any patterns or situations that seem to be associated with difficult emotions. For example, you may notice that social situations or work deadlines tend to trigger feelings of anxiety, while spending time in nature or engaging in creative activities helps you feel more relaxed and content.

Once you've identified your triggers, you can begin to develop strategies for managing them. This may involve avoiding or minimizing exposure to triggers when possible, such as setting boundaries around work or social obligations, or finding ways to cope with triggers when they do arise, such as practicing relaxation techniques or engaging in self-soothing activities like listening to music or taking a warm bath.

Another effective strategy for managing triggers is to practice cognitive-behavioral techniques, such as reframing negative thoughts and challenging limiting beliefs. This may involve working with a mental health professional to identify and challenge negative thought patterns, or using self-help resources such as books or online courses to learn new cognitive-behavioral skills.

Ultimately, managing triggers requires a combination of self-awareness, self-care, and proactive planning. By identifying potential triggers, developing effective coping strategies, and prioritizing self-care, individuals can minimize the impact of triggers on their mental health and wellbeing and maintain a greater sense of control and resilience in their daily lives.

Planning for the future and maintaining hope

Planning for the future and maintaining hope is an important part of finding meaning and purpose in life, and can be particularly helpful for individuals who have experienced depression or suicidal thoughts. By setting goals and making plans for the future, individuals can create a sense of purpose and direction, and develop a greater sense of hope and optimism.

One strategy for planning for the future is to set SMART goals, which are specific, measurable, achievable, relevant, and time-bound. For example, a SMART goal might be to enroll in a class or training program that will help you develop new skills and advance in your career, or to plan a trip or vacation that will give you something to look forward to and help you recharge and rejuvenate.

In addition to setting goals, it's important to cultivate a sense of hope and optimism about the future. This may involve practicing gratitude and focusing on the positive aspects of your life, cultivating a sense of purpose and meaning, and seeking out support and connection with others.

One effective strategy for maintaining hope is to focus on the things that are within your control, and to take small, concrete steps toward your goals each day. This may involve breaking larger goals down into smaller, manageable steps, and celebrating each small victory along the way.

Ultimately, planning for the future and maintaining hope requires a combination of self-awareness, resilience, and proactive planning. By setting goals, cultivating a positive mindset, and focusing on the things that are within their control, individuals can develop a sense of purpose and direction, and maintain a greater sense of hope and optimism about the future.

Conclusion

In conclusion, "Choosing Life: Finding Meaning and Reasons to Stay Alive" is a comprehensive guide for individuals who are struggling with depression, anxiety, or suicidal thoughts, as well as their loved ones and caregivers. Through exploring the impact of suicide on individuals, families, and communities, examining inner thoughts and emotions, and developing coping skills and strategies for managing triggers, readers can gain a deeper understanding of their mental health and develop effective tools for maintaining wellness and resilience.

The book also emphasizes the importance of creating a support system, both through seeking out professional help and connecting with community resources such as support groups and other communities. Additionally, by identifying personal values and goals, pursuing passions and interests, and planning for the future, individuals can develop a sense of purpose and meaning that can help them stay motivated and focused on their recovery.

Ultimately, "Choosing Life" provides a roadmap for individuals who are seeking to improve their mental health and find meaning and reasons to stay alive. By recognizing the impact of suicide, exploring inner thoughts and emotions, developing coping skills and resilience, building a support system, and creating a sustainable plan for life, individuals can take steps to maintain wellness and hope, and build a fulfilling and meaningful life.

www.ingramcontent.com/pod-product-compliance
Lightning Source LLC
Chambersburg PA
CBHW061606250726
48657CB00017B/2209